Otto Von Schnoodle™

Grace Birch

# The Adventures of
# Otto Von Schnoodle™

## Otto's Neighborhood Heroes

### Police

### Firefighters

### EMT Paramedics

*Dedicated to all the men and women who serve and protect...*

*Every day placing others before themselves. Thank You!*

Published by Grace Birch, Printed in the United States of America

First Edition

Library of Congress Cataloging-in-Publication Data available upon request

ISBN-10: 0996480447 Hardcover       ISBN-13: 978-0-9964804-4-4 Hardcover

Editing by Kathleen Given

Jacket Design by Vince Pannullo

**Grace Birch** lives in Southwest Florida with her husband and beloved dog, Otto Von Schnoodle. She summers in Maine, where she grew up. Grace has been an avid animal lover her entire life, always with a furry friend or two at her feet. She is also a big supporter of many pet shelters and rescues.

A teacher by trade, Grace understands the importance of reading to children. Grace worked for several years as an instructor with a major U.S. airline, realizing comprehension, of any subject matter, is greatly dependent on a person's ability to read and write. Grace believes you can never start too early with children and hopes her Otto series will engage and excite!

Grace invites you to visit Otto's website where you can join his **Read With Otto** program and stay apprised of upcoming book signings, charitable events and book releases.

www.TheAdventuresOfOttoVonSchnoodle.com

# *Police*

Otto heard a strange beeping sound from outside. He was playing checkers with Sock Monkey and was about to win, but the noise kept getting louder so they stopped playing.

Otto ran to the window and saw a very large truck. He had never seen a truck like this before.

He ran down the hall looking for Mommy, but couldn't find her. Otto went out to the back porch and saw her picking flowers. He immediately thought of Dugan and the beautiful flowers he grew in his garden. He and Frankie were heading over to visit Dolly and Dugan later this afternoon.

"Mommy, what is that big truck doing next door?" Otto asked.

"We are getting new neighbors," Mommy replied. "That is why I am picking flowers.  As soon as I'm done, we will walk over and say hello. Go brush your teeth, comb your hair, and then get Allie and Sock Monkey.  I'll be right in."

Otto thought about that for a minute. He was excited to have new neighbors. He loved people and was not afraid of strangers, as long as Mommy and Daddy gave their approval. ✓

Otto turned and ran back inside to get ready. Allie and Sock Monkey were reading their books on the couch.

Mommy came back with the flowers and picked up the basket of cookies that was sitting on the counter.

"Let's go!" she said. Otto, Allie, and Sock Monkey followed her out the back door and over the lawn to the neighbor's driveway.

What Otto saw next made him stop in his tracks; a very large dog, sitting inside a dark blue car, and another dog sitting beside a man wearing a big brimmed hat.

Two more cars, both with writing all over them, were parked in the driveway. There were three men in total - two with dogs, one without - all talking to each other.

It appeared the two with dogs were getting ready to leave, as Otto could hear them saying goodbye to one another.

Otto squinted a bit. He was able to see that one of the dogs was also wearing a badge.

Before Otto, Allie, Sock Monkey, and Mommy got much closer, the two men with dogs got into their cars, buckled their seatbelts, and drove away with a wave.

The third man, with no hat and no dog, walked up to Otto and said, "Hi, I'm Officer Milt. What is your name?"

Otto backed up, ears lowered. He had never seen clothes or cars like this before. He started to shake with fear.

"Don't be afraid. I won't hurt you. I am a police officer and my job is to help people. I wear a uniform to help you identify me. If you are ever in trouble, you can look for someone wearing clothes like mine and you'll know everything will be okay."

He extended his hand with a big, wonderful smile on his face. Otto looked over at Mommy and she nodded her head yes.

"I'm Otto Von Schnoodle and these are my friends: Sock Monkey and Allie," Otto said. "We brought you some flowers and cookies to welcome you to the neighborhood."

"Why, thank you. That is very nice of you," Officer Milt said, taking the gifts from Mommy.

"Would you like to take a look inside my car?"

Otto, Sock Monkey, and Allie all nodded their heads up and down.
Otto ran over to the car and jumped in, with Allie
and Sock Monkey right behind him.

They saw all sorts of fun things in the car, including a computer.

"Officer Milt, why do you have a computer in your car?" Otto asked.

"Well, Otto, sometimes there is information we need quickly,
so a computer is very helpful."

"Can we see?" asked Otto.

Officer Milt opened the computer and Allie jumped up onto the keyboard. She didn't want to miss a thing.

Just then Officer Milt's phone rang.

"Otto, I must take this phone call. Please excuse me."

Otto, Sock Monkey, and Allie waited patiently.

Once Officer Milt was done with his phone call, Otto asked, "Who were those men with the dogs? Their cars have the same writing on them as your car."

"That was Officer Josh with his partner Matrix, and Trooper Cooley with his partner, Bruin."

"Do you have a partner?" Otto asked sheepishly.

"No, I don't. Would you like to be my partner, Otto?"

Otto couldn't believe what he was hearing. He had never been a partner before, but he really liked the idea.

"Well, Otto, we are about to have our first ride together!
That was the reason for the phone call.
Would you like to go with me to see what's going on?"

Otto was so excited he jumped out of the car and ran over to Mommy,
telling her that he was now Officer Milt's partner and
they needed to respond to a call.

Mommy said he could go, so he ran back to the car and jumped in.

Officer Milt held Otto in his lap, with Allie still on the computer.
They weren't going far, just around the corner.

"I have a friend named Buster. I bet he would like to help.
You know, for when you need two partners," Otto said,
just as Officer Milt brought the car to a stop.

# *Firefighters*

Once the car was parked, Officer Milt, Otto, Sock Monkey, and Allie got out.

There were two things that immediately caught Otto's attention, the first being a flock of chickens wandering around on the lawn. They looked very scared and were clucking loudly.

The second being two red trucks with flashing lights.
He had never seen anything like it before.

There were lots of people walking around in really strange outfits. They were similar, yet different, from Officer Milt's uniform.

One of the trucks had backed up to a tree with the ladder extended.
Why? Otto wondered.

Otto and Officer Milt walked over to the ladder and looked up. There, stuck in the tree, was a chicken crying and calling out for help.

Otto paced frantically. He was so upset the chicken was up the tree. He looked at Officer Milt with pleading eyes asking, "Can you help him?"

Sock Monkey and Allie came running over. They now understood why the chickens on the ground were clucking so loudly.

**Please Help**

**Me !**

While they were standing there, one of men climbed up the ladder,
bent over, and started talking to the chicken.
Otto could hear him saying everything would be okay.

"It will be alright, I promise," said Officer Milt.
"Look, they are bringing the chicken down now."

Just as Officer Milt spoke, Otto looked over his shoulder to see the man
walking down the ladder, holding the chicken.

"Is he a policeman?" Otto asked.

"No, Otto, he is a firefighter," said Officer Milt. "We all work together. Firefighters are trained to put out fires and to rescue people and animals from danger."

"Do they have partners, like you?" Otto asked.

"Sometimes they love to have partners. Sometimes they can't have partners. It all depends on what they are doing. I bet today they would love for you to be their partner. Let's go see."

They walked towards the truck. Another firefighter, a lady, met them at the bottom of the ladder. She turned and smiled.

"Natalie, I would like to introduce you to my new friends," Officer Milt said. "This is Otto and he would like to know if he could help you today and be your partner. There is one problem, however. Your equipment and uniforms are making him very nervous."

"Hi, Otto," said Natalie. "It's nice to meet you. Yes, we would love for you to help us today. Please don't be afraid of our gear. All this funny clothing and equipment helps us help you. Let me get you a fire hat to wear, like mine, then we can climb up the ladder to meet Adam and the rescued chicken."

Otto was so excited! Now that he understood the reason for the equipment, he was no longer afraid. He couldn't believe what fun he was having. He extended his paw to Adam and the chicken.
"Hi, I am Otto. Would you like to be my friend?"

The chicken - looking less fearful now that he was out of the tree - said, "Hi, I'm Caleb. Nice to meet you, Otto!
Yes, I would love to be your friend."

# EMT/Paramedics

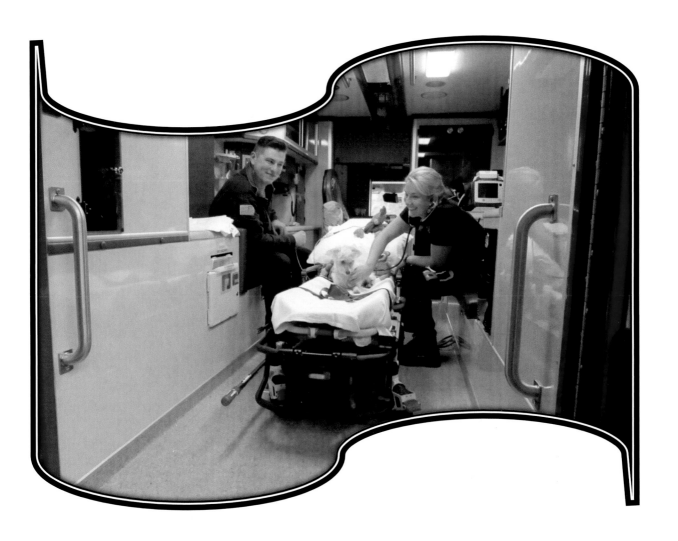

"Caleb," said Adam, "How are you feeling? Do you hurt anywhere?"

Caleb, looking very relieved to be on the ground, said sheepishly, "No, I don't think I'm hurt. I don't know what happened. We were all playing and somehow I flew into the tree. But then I couldn't get down. My family called 9-1-1 and, thankfully, you came and saved me."

"That's what we are here for," said Natalie. "Let's give you a quick check-up. Do you see that fun red truck over there? It has all sorts of wonderful equipment that helps make sure you are alright.
How about if you, Otto, Allie, and Sock Monkey get in?"

Everybody looked at each other, and then raced to the back of the truck. Adam opened the door and they all jumped in.

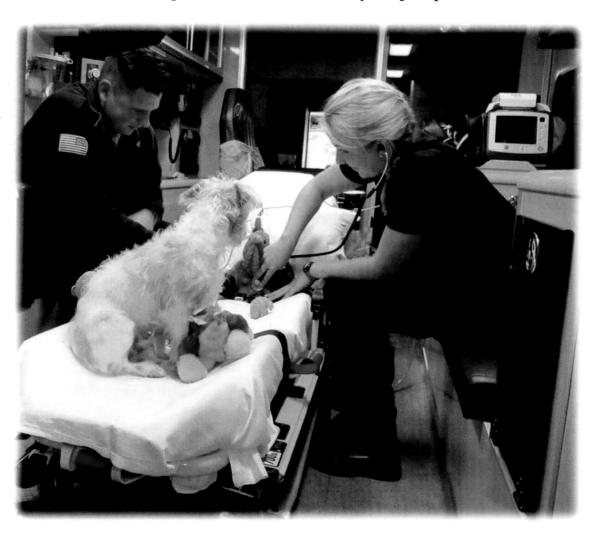

"First, let's listen to your heart with my stethoscope," said Natalie.

She pulled out a funny looking instrument, putting one end in her ears and placing the other end on Caleb's chest.

Otto, looking on very anxiously, asked, "Does it hurt?"

"No, it doesn't hurt at all," said Natalie. "Would you like me to listen to your heart, Otto?"

Otto, who had been sitting at the foot of the bed, jumped up and sat closer to Natalie.

Caleb climbed up onto the pillow.

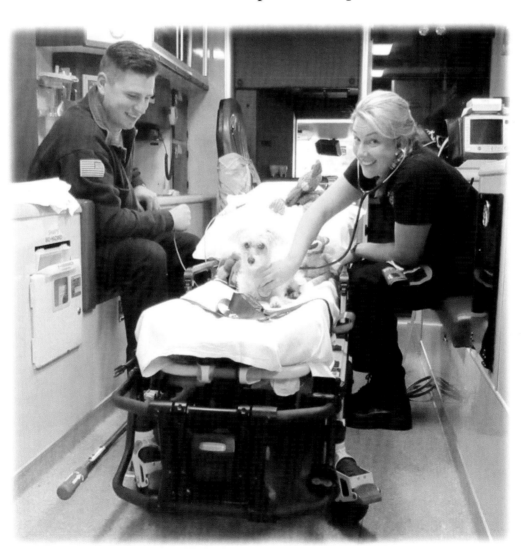

Adam and Natalie smiled.
"You both check out perfectly," they said together.

Otto stood up and asked, "Can you take us back up on the ladder?"

Caleb, hearing this, began squawking loudly. He wanted nothing to do with going up the ladder now that he was firmly back on level ground.

"You three go," he said. "I will stay down here and wait for you."

Everyone laughed. Natalie and Adam grabbed Otto, Allie and Sock Monkey, and headed toward the ladder.

Otto was having the time of his life. And of course, Sock Monkey, who loved to climb trees, thought it was the most fun he'd had in a long time. Allie held on tightly to Adam's coat.

Officer Milt yelled up to Otto,

"How do you like being a volunteer firefighter?"

"It's the best! Will you take our picture?"

"Absolutely! Say cheese!"

Officer Milt clicked away with his camera.

Once they had their pictures taken, Otto looked at Caleb and said,
"Would you like to come home with us?
You can meet the rest of my friends and family."

Caleb nodded. He was so grateful to all these wonderful men and
women who had saved him.
He was also very excited to have new friends.

"Yes, I would love that!"

"Alright, then, let's get in the car!" said Officer Milt.

They all jumped in and buckled up.

Everybody waved to Natalie, Adam, and the rest of the firefighters and
paramedics. Officer Milt turned on his blue lights and siren,
then away they went, headed home.

As soon as the car stopped, Allie and Sock Monkey, along with Caleb, jumped out and headed towards Mommy.

Otto jumped into Officer Milt's lap.

"I had such fun today! Where would we be without the police, firefighters, and EMT?
And to think I can help out from time to time, being your partner!"

"Thank you, Otto. It makes me happy you are no longer afraid of our uniforms or us. We are always here to help you, your friends, and your family," said Officer Milt.

"Before you go, Otto, there is something I would like to give you."

Officer Milt opened the glove box of the car and pulled out
two badges, along with two black shirts.

"These are for you and Buster."

"Oh, Officer Milt, I love you," Otto said.
He then leaned up and gave him a kiss.

Everyone was talking at the same time, trying to tell Mommy and Branch all about their Adventure.

"I have an idea," Mommy said. "Why don't you call Buster, Dolly, Dugan, and Frankie and invite them for dinner. They would love to hear all about today's Adventure."

After dinner, Otto and Buster put on their new shirts. They fit perfectly! Daddy pinned on their badges and made an announcement:

***"I hereby pronounce Otto and Buster official police, firefighter and EMT partners, helping those men and women who help us!"***

Everyone clapped!! Dolly brought the cake to the table. When Mommy cut into it, all sorts of fun candy fell out! A piñata cake! What fun!

Otto couldn't believe it….. another magical Adventure!

Heartfelt thanks to the wonderful men and women of the Cumberland Police Department, Cumberland Fire and Rescue Department, Yarmouth Police Department, and Maine State Police, for assisting us with this project.

# Otto's 9-1-1 Guide

If you think you are in trouble, or anyone around you is in trouble or hurt, dial 9-1-1. Information below will help them help you.

**STAY CALM     SPEAK SLOWLY     DO NOT HANG UP**

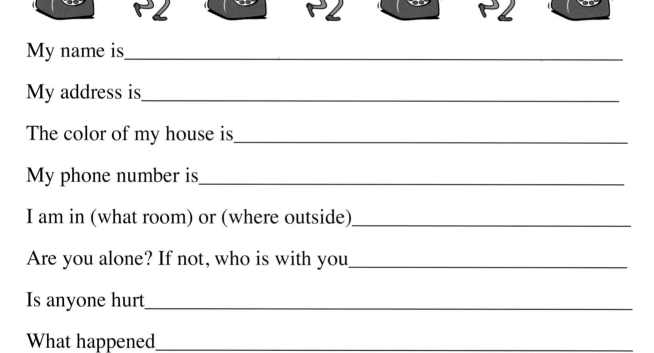

My name is_____

My address is_____

The color of my house is_____

My phone number is_____

I am in (what room) or (where outside)_____

Are you alone? If not, who is with you_____

Is anyone hurt_____

What happened_____

## NEVER CALL 9-1-1 UNLESS IT IS A REAL EMERGENCY

### IF AN ADULT IS AVAILABLE, ASK THEM TO HELP YOU

# *My Schnoodle Doodle Page*